GABRIEL FAURÉ
VOCALISES

Voice and Piano / Chant et piano / Singstimme und Klavier

Critical edition by / Édition critique de / Kritische Ausgabe von

Roy Howat · Emily Kilpatrick

Urtext

First edition / Première publication / Erstveröffentlichung

EIGENTUM DES VERLEGERS · ALLE RECHTE VORBEHALTEN
ALL RIGHTS RESERVED

PETERS EDITION LTD

A member of the EDITION PETERS GROUP
FRANKFURT/M. · LEIPZIG · LONDON · NEW YORK

Cover Painting:
Leaving the Conservatoire, 1899 (oil on canvas), Beraud, Jean (1849–1935)
Musee de la Ville de Paris, Musee Carnavalet, Paris, France / Giraudon
The Bridgeman Art Library XIR 19978

© 2013 by Peters Edition Ltd, London

Alle Rechte vorbehalten · All rights reserved
Vervielfältigungen jeglicher Art sind gesetzlich verboten.
Any unauthorized reproduction is prohibited by law.

ISMN 979-0-014-11441-1

Gabriel Fauré's vocal art consists mainly of a richly varied corpus of songs, or "*mélodies*". For recital singers these are an absolute "must", distinct from those of Debussy in being less literary-based and more "instrumental" – as is borne out by the many instrumental adaptations of some of Fauré's best-known songs (most famously "Après un rêve").

The rediscovery here of Fauré's Vocalises (of which only one has hitherto been available), magnificently presented by Roy Howat and Emily Kilpatrick, offers singers an incomparable gateway into Fauré's very personal and specific vocal art, quite independent of poetic texts, yet stylistically instantly recognisable.

Far from being just another contribution to vocal and musical training, this constitutes an important body of art, in a field mostly neglected by the great composers. Both as a great composer, and in his role as Director of France's National Conservatoire of Music, Fauré takes full command here.

Singing teachers, I am certain, will be thrilled by this discovery; and the order of presentation chosen (by progressive musical and vocal demands) will help each singer to comprehend and stylistically serve the unique figure that Fauré presents in French musical literature.

François Le Roux
Artistic Director, Académie Francis Poulenc

Dans l'œuvre de Gabriel Fauré, le corpus vocal est constitué principalement de « mélodies ». Un « must » pour les récitalistes servant le genre, totalement différent dans la forme de ce que Debussy a accompli dans le même domaine, car d'une approche bien plus instrumentale que littéraire. Ce qui a d'ailleurs conduit à de nombreuses adaptations de certaines des mélodies les plus connues de Fauré pour violon, violoncelle, ou autres instruments (par exemple le très fameux « Après un rêve »).

L'identification et la redécouverte, magnifiquement présentées ici par Roy Howat et Emily Kilpatrick, de ces « Vocalises » (dont une seulement était jusqu'ici disponible), ouvrent aux chanteurs une porte d'accès incomparable à l'univers vocal si particulier de Fauré, totalement indépendante des textes poétiques, et pourtant toujours reconnaissable.

Il ne s'agit pas d'un apport mineur au travail vocal et musical, mais au contraire d'une œuvre d'art au sens propre, dans un répertoire qui est d'habitude bien négligé par les grands compositeurs. Fauré prend ici sa tâche à bras le corps, à la fois en tant que Directeur du Conservatoire National de Musique et en grand compositeur.

Les professeurs de chant seront, j'en suis sûr, enchantés de la découverte ; et la présentation ici choisie (par ordre croissant de difficulté vocale et musicale) aidera chaque chanteur à comprendre et à servir stylistiquement la figure singulière de Fauré dans la littérature musicale française.

François Le Roux
Directeur artistique, Académie Francis Poulenc

Gabriel Faurés Vokalschaffen besteht im Wesentlichen aus „*Mélodies*", die ein „Must" für alle Konzertsänger darstellen. Im Unterschied zum Liedschaffen Debussys sind sie weniger vom Textinhalt her als vielmehr „instrumental" empfunden, was im Übrigen zu verschiedenen Bearbeitungen einiger der bekanntesten Lieder Faurés für Viola, Cello oder andere Instrumente geführt hat (darunter beispielsweise das berühmte „Après un rêve").

Die Wiederentdeckung der „Vokalisen" (bisher war nur eine einzige überhaupt zugänglich) und die vorliegende, von Roy Howat und Emily Kilpatrick hervorragend edierte Ausgabe eröffnen Sängerinnen und Sängern einen einzigartigen Zugang zu Faurés so charakteristischer Vokalkunst: völlig losgelöst von dichterischen Vorlagen und doch stets unverkennbar.

Es handelt sich hierbei keineswegs um Gelegenheitswerke für die sängerische und musikalische Arbeit; Vokalisen bilden im Gegenteil ein eigenständiges Genre innerhalb eines Repertoires, das von den großen Komponisten gewöhnlich vernachlässigt wird. Fauré aber wird dieser Aufgabe gleich zweifach gerecht: als Direktor des Conservatoire National de Musique und zugleich als einer der bedeutendsten Komponisten seiner Zeit.

Gesangspädagogen werden – da bin ich mir sicher – von dieser Wiederentdeckung begeistert sein. Dank der vorliegenden Erstausgabe der Vokalisen (in progressiver Reihenfolge und nach musikalischem und sängerischem Schwierigkeitsgrad angeordnet), wird jede Sängerin, jeder Sänger die stilistische Einzigartigkeit der Tonsprache Faurés und ihren besonderen Stellenwert in der französischen Musikliteratur nachempfinden können.

François Le Roux
Künstlerischer Direktor, Académie Francis Poulenc

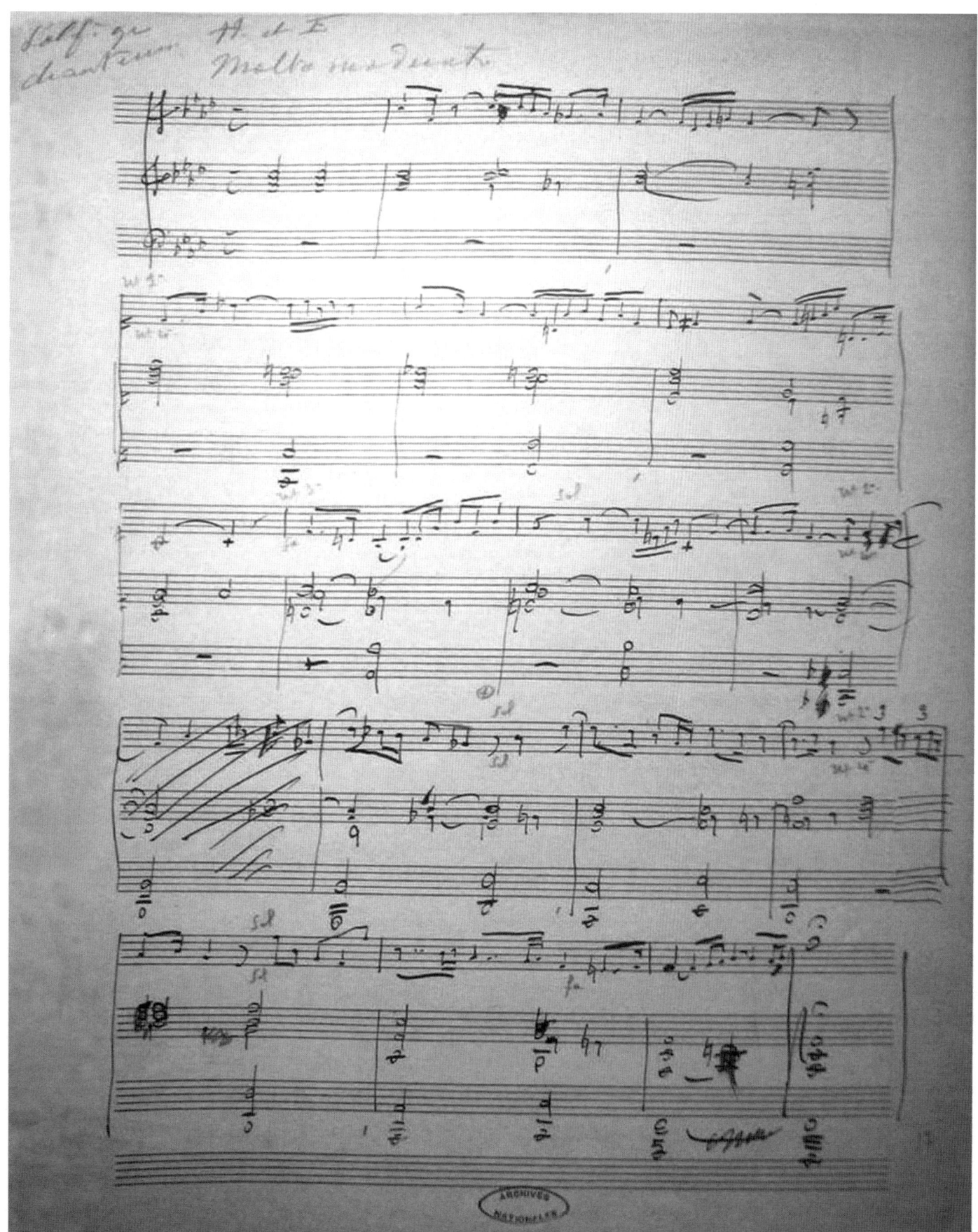

Gabriel Fauré
Vocalise in F minor / *fa* mineur / f-Moll, no. [24]
Solfège chanteurs · H.[ommes] et F.[emmes] · Molto moderato

Autograph manuscript, June 1916, showing revisions by the composer
Manuscrit autographe, juin 1916, montrant des révisions du compositeur
Autographe Niederschrift, Juni 1916, mit Korrekturen des Komponisten

Archives nationales (AJ[37] 201.3), Pierrefitte-sur-Seine, France
Reproduced by permission

Preface

When Gabriel Fauré was appointed Director of the Paris Conservatoire in 1905, one of his most pressing concerns – and first achievements – was a complete reform of the teaching of singing. He was determined to steer the singing courses away from a long-entrenched obsession with second-rate grand opera (Auber, Halévy and the like), and to introduce mandatory study of art song, along with "exercises developing vocal suppleness, articulation and voice placement and production, which are the basis of singing teaching".[1] To this end, between 1906 and 1916 he composed a substantial body of accompanied vocalises for use in the Conservatoire's sight-singing examinations. For a century these vocalises – now held in the Archives nationales de France – have lain unknown to the musical world at large. Their first publication here marks a major event for the vocal teaching repertoire (as well as some entrancing music); a marvellous resource of skilfully devised vocal exercises ranging from elementary to advanced virtuoso level, all from one of history's greatest song composers.

With habitual modesty about his own output, Fauré never planned his Conservatoire vocalises for publication. Taken in chronological order they fluctuate unpredictably in technical difficulty, perhaps reflecting the varying quality of student talent year by year.[2] Male and female students at that time were given separate tests (as were singers and instrumentalists), and the vocalises Fauré devised for each category mostly suggest that he not only regarded the female voice as more nimble than its male counterpart, but also expected more agility again from instrumentalists, judging by no. [29]. Since the purpose of these vocalises was practical from the outset, as with the present edition, they are ordered here progressively by level of difficulty, rather than chronologically. Despite their professedly humble purpose, many of them show Fauré's inspiration taking sudden flight (particularly from around no. [20] onwards), on a level with his best songs.

Exceptionally, no. [28] was composed for publication, in a collection of *Vocalises-Études* compiled, possibly at Fauré's instigation, by voice professor Amédée-Louis Hettich.[3] For his compendium Hettich commissioned contributions from composers including Dukas, d'Indy, Hahn, Koechlin, Ravel and Ropartz; Fauré's own contribution opens the first volume, published early in 1907. The similar date of the present no. [29], along with other aspects of its manuscript presentation, suggests that this extraordinary cantilena may also have been originally devised for Hettich's collection but deemed too difficult – and foisted instead on the Conservatoire examinees most capable of surviving it! This vocalise stands out in Fauré's whole output, bearing witness to how steeped he was in the art of J. S. Bach.

It was customary for Conservatoire professors to share the composition of examination tests over any year. During his tenure as Director, Fauré – who in earlier years had contributed pieces respectively for cello, flute, piano, violin, and harp[4] – concentrated on sight-singing tests, delegating the task to colleagues when his schedule was otherwise preoccupied with concerts or major composing projects. The surviving collection of examination vocalises shows pronounced stylistic contrasts across the contributions by different composers, but most strongly between Fauré's and any others.[5] Fauré's invariably start more simply, usually by making the singer pitch a triad, and avoid the habitual operatic roulades, clichés and distracting keyboard figurations: in the process they quietly but surely (and sometimes mischievously) probe the candidate's vocal and musical skills.

The Appendices

These qualities bear crucially on a group of sixteen Conservatoire vocalises from the years 1910–15, which survive only in official copies that leave the composer unnamed. Several factors strongly suggest these too are by Fauré, and support their inclusion here as Appendix 1. Their style is very much that of Fauré's authenticated vocalises, and far from that of all the other identified contributors of vocalises. They also comprise the only such unattributed ensemble of vocalises, the Conservatoire having normally preserved the original manuscripts of other contributors (which, unlike Fauré's, were usually signed by their authors) and identified them on scribal copies. Such apparent breaches of protocol would be most naturally explained by the author of the unattributed pieces being the institution's own Director. The pieces in question being mostly on the shorter and simpler side, their autographs, probably written on odd scraps of manuscript paper, may have been lost or even discarded after copying. Several of these pieces show unmistakable Fauré hallmarks, such as the modal surprises or sequences in the middle of nos. [ii], [x] and [xi]; sudden octave leaps at the end of a piece (as in several of Fauré's authenticated vocalises); or strategically-placed deceptive, interrupted or otherwise booby-trapped cadences that can easily throw the inattentive singer – not least in the closing bars of no. [xvi]. The rising scale from the tonic that opens nos. [iv], [vii] and [xii] is also a thoroughly characteristic Fauré gambit (see, for example, no. [28]). These vocalises again are ranged here in technically progressive order to let them serve the same purpose as the main body of vocalises. Appendix 2 reproduces dictation tests devised by Fauré in 1907 and 1909, which can usefully serve as unaccompanied vocal exercises.

Musical characteristics

As already noted, Fauré's vocalises quietly test and develop both musicality and vocal skill, in more focussed ways than the florid exercises that were long the norm. Usually starting with exposed triadic intervals, they then probe essentials such as breath control, purity of tone and stability of pitch and rhythm, sometimes over distracting modal shifts in the accompaniment. The texturally simple keyboard accompaniments oblige singers to find their way from note to note mostly unaided by leading figurations, with progressively trickier vocal intervals and unintuitive melodic progressions to be negotiated. With no phrasing marked in most of the manuscripts, sight-singing students had to use their wits and read ahead to judge and shape phrase lengths, particularly when Fauré prolongs a melody or suddenly transfers it up an octave just as it seems about to relax into a cadence. In a similar spirit are enharmonic hazards, such as the E♭ tied to a D♯ in no. [25] (a trap Fauré also laid in instrumental sight-reading test pieces). This particular vocalise epitomises Fauré's penchant for modal and enharmonic play, its first four bars veering from A♭ to C♭ major and back (like the first harmonic move in *La Bonne Chanson*), before the B[7] harmony in bar 7 sets off an enharmonic pun against the C♭ of bar 3.[6]

While Conservatoire vocalises by other composers mostly mimic the *bel canto* aria, Fauré's sound much more like *mélodies*, with distinctly Fauréan gestures or turns of phrase in even the simplest ones, as well as some more overt echoes such as those of *Lydia* in no. [20]. All this complements and supports his introduction of art song as fundamental to the Conservatoire singing curriculum. In a letter written shortly before his retirement, Fauré reaffirmed that his reforms to the teaching of singing were among his proudest achievements as Director, singling out the emphasis on technical training and the importance of *solfège*.[7] The challenges posed by his collected vocalises are as potent and vital for singers today as they were a century ago.

Performing suggestions

Fauré's vocalises serve two important purposes. In their original guise as sight-singing tests, they demand and develop acute aural awareness, vocal placement and musical alertness. More extended study can instil and develop accuracy of intonation, purity of tone, articulation and breath control, while the pieces' modal adventurousness, supple melodic lines and fluidity of phrasing make them ideal preparation for artsong in general, and the genre of French *mélodie* in particular.

Exactly how Fauré or the Conservatoire examiners intended them to be vocalised remains unspecified. At least some of them may have been "solfèged" in the traditional French manner, but this is barely possible in the more advanced ones (notably no. [29]); perhaps just some of the simpler ones were intended for "solfèging", as may have been specified on the occasion. The most useful indications in this regard come from Hettich's *"Petite préface"* to the compendium of *Vocalises-Études* that opens with Fauré's contribution (the present no. [28]):

> These vocalises are generally to be sung on the vowel *a*: but all those who practise singing, teachers and students, know that *a* in the voice is as varied as green in the countryside and blue in the sky. According to the individual voice and according to registers, the *a* thus can take on a circumflex or grave accent, thus colouring itself with a degree of *o* and *e*. It will even prove useful, frankly, to use these vowels in conjunction with *a* in a single vocalise. A strongly dental *e*, a variant of the normal *e*, will efficiently correct any guttural or muted emission.
>
> [...] To progress gradually to the tensing and bringing together of the [vocal] cords, as demanded by laryngeal physiology, it is often useful and prudent to precede the emitted vowel by one of the plosive consonants: *m–b–p*, corresponding to the dynamic degrees ***p–mf–f***. Guttural or muted voices can employ *v* which will ensure the vital participation of the teeth and lips.

Besides practising with different vowel and consonant sounds, performers may wish to experiment with different phrase divisions, shapings and dynamic colourings. The phrasing marked by Fauré on nos. [20] and [28] has been taken here as a model for editorial breathing commas added to the remaining vocalises. These should be regarded as suggestions, those in parentheses present merely in case of need. Vocalises with no tempo heading can be studied at different tempi (this indeed can apply to any of them), working up gently to a flowing (sometimes quite nimble) tempo without sacrificing steadiness of tempo or accuracy of rhythm and pitch. Fauré was famously a stickler in these respects, his insistence on keeping in time balanced by distaste for any heaviness in tempi, as well as by a strong aversion to any kind of swooning effects or sentimental lingering.

Given the multifarious challenges these pieces pose, an exact order of technical difficulty must remain somewhat debatable. Some clear progressions are evident, however (independent of the pieces' chronology), for example through the sequential figurations in nos. [7–9], and more generally through their ever-increasing demands for vocal and rhythmic nimbleness, in negotiating contrasted or unexpected intervals, or in maintaining pitch stability in the teeth of unpredictable modal onslaughts from the accompaniment. (Nos. [25] onward provide some exhilaratingly wild rides in that respect.) For practical purposes, an editorial summary of perceived challenges through the vocalises is provided here on page XIV.

Editorial note

The manuscripts of Fauré's vocalises offer a rare glimpse into his busy working life. Never having been prepared for publication, the twenty-eight surviving Conservatoire autographs appear to be final working drafts that doubled as fair copies. Some shorter, less challenging ones were probably dashed off during busy weeks in the office; others suggest a sudden inspiration taking Fauré by surprise; and a few evince considerable thought and preparation, perhaps in developing a musical concept from an existing repository of material. (One or two are written on the reverse of draft pages for works like the Fifth Impromptu and *Pénélope*.) Reworkings visible on several manuscripts bear witness to the care Fauré took over them. In particular, the closing portion of no. [29] shows a revision probably aimed at clarifying its continuity of line; even so, Fauré's earlier reading of the passage is so remarkable (and vocally useful) that it is also printed here.

Tempo headings appear only where sources supply them. The exceptional rhythmic challenges of no. [29] have prompted an editorial metronomic suggestion. Anything in square brackets is editorial; cautionary accidentals in parentheses appear thus in the sources. Editorial ties and slurs are printed in broken lines. All phrasing is editorial except in nos. [20] and [28].

Acknowledgments

The editors warmly thank those who have helped the preparation of the present edition: Mme Yvette Isselin of the Archives nationales de France; Mmes Anne Bongrain, Bérengère de l'Epine and Marie-Hélène Coudroy-Saghaï of the Paris Conservatoire; Mme Dominique Hausfater and M. Yann Mével of the Conservatoire's Médiathèque Hector Berlioz; the music staff at the Bibliothèque nationale de France in Paris; and the many performing and teaching colleagues who have provided supportive enthusiasm, expertise and invaluable musical feedback. The editors gratefully acknowledge the Arts and Humanities Research Council (UK), in supporting the research for the present edition through a Project Grant based at the Royal Academy of Music, London.

London, 2013 *Roy Howat & Emily Kilpatrick*

---

[1] Letter of 5 November 1905, Étienne Dujardin-Beaumetz (Under-Secretary of State for Fine Arts) to Fauré, comprising a Directive from the Ministry of Education and Fine Arts, whose wording was almost certainly prompted by Fauré himself; Archives nationales de France, AJ[37] 84/6. The directive specifies that the first year of Conservatoire vocal training be devoted almost exclusively to study of exercises and

vocalises. For full transcriptions of official documentation relating to Fauré's reforms, and for details of relevant Conservatoire examination procedures, see Anne Bongrain, *Le Conservatoire National de Musique et de Déclamation 1900–1930: Documents historiques et administratifs* (Paris, 2012), pp. 17–23, 41, 75–77 and 84–87.

[2] Variations in technical level also reflect the vocalises having been devised for different exams over the Conservatoire year (though even that yields less than consistent grading, and existing tests were also sometimes reused for different exams in later years). The standard exams were for Admission (October/November), mid-year exams in January/February and May, and the competitive end-of-year *concours* in June/July.

[3] *Répertoire Moderne de Vocalises-Etudes*, publiées sous la direction de A. L. Hettich, Professeur au Conservatoire (Paris, Editions Alphonse Leduc, 1907–); originally planned as 3 volumes, the series had run to seven large volumes (56 fascicules) by the time of Hettich's death in 1937, with Messiaen and Poulenc among the later contributors.

[4] The sight-reading pieces in question for cello, flute, piano and violin are published in Peters editions EP 7571, 7514, 7601 (comprising Fauré's *Pièces brèves* for piano) and 7515.

[5] Other composers of Conservatoire sight-singing tests between 1905 and Fauré's retirement in 1920 included Georges Caussade, Émile Pessard, Marcel Chadeigne, Henri Busser, J. Morpain, Jules Mouquet, Eugène Piffaretti, Paul Rougnon, Paul Vidal, and Jacques and Louise Samuel-Rousseau. Most of these also contributed to Hettich's compendium.

[6] The vocal lines of these vocalises, for their original exam usage, were also barbed with clef changes, mostly involving moveable C-clefs (an element omitted from the present edition). Fauré's pedagogical rigour – along perhaps with his native sense of mischief – is apparent in his positioning of these clef changes: whereas his colleagues tended to position them helpfully after phrase-ends, Fauré as often as not changes them in mid-phrase and across tricky intervals. Not for nothing was one of his Conservatoire nicknames "Robespierre".

[7] Letter to Paul Léon, 26 December 1919, quoted in Jean-Michel Nectoux, "Gabriel Fauré au Conservatoire de Paris: Une philosophie pour l'enseignement", in *Le Conservatoire de Paris: Des Menus-Plaisirs à la Cité de la musique, 1795–1995*, ed. Anne Bongrain and Yves Gérard (Paris: Éditions Buchet/Chastel, 1996), p. 221.

Préface

Quand Gabriel Fauré fut nommé directeur du Conservatoire de Paris en 1905, l'une de ses préoccupations les plus urgentes – et l'une de ses premières réalisations – fut une réforme complète de l'enseignement du chant. Il était en effet résolu à détourner les cours de chant du grand opéra de second rang (Auber, Halévy et consorts), devenu depuis longtemps une obsession, et à imposer l'étude de la mélodie, avec des « exercices d'assouplissement vocal, de pose de la voix, d'articulation et d'émission qui sont la base de l'enseignement du chant[1] ». À cette fin, entre 1906 et 1916, il composa un ensemble substantiel de vocalises accompagnées destinées aux examens de déchiffrage du Conservatoire. Pendant un siècle, ces vocalises – conservées aux Archives nationales de France – sont restées méconnues du monde musical. Leur première publication ici est un événement majeur pour le répertoire vocal didactique (avec quelques pages ravissantes) : c'est un merveilleux ensemble d'exercices vocaux habilement conçus, qui vont du niveau élémentaire à la virtuosité avancée, tous dus à l'un des plus grands compositeurs de mélodies de l'histoire.

Avec sa modestie habituelle s'agissant de ses propres compositions, Fauré n'a jamais destiné à la publication ses vocalises écrites pour le Conservatoire. Prises par ordre chronologique, elles sont d'une difficulté technique fluctuante et imprévisible, reflétant peut-être le niveau variable des élèves d'une année sur l'autre[2]. À cette époque, les élèves masculins et féminins (aussi bien chanteurs qu'instrumentistes) avaient des épreuves séparées, et les vocalises que Fauré conçut pour chacune des deux catégories semblent indiquer en général que non seulement il considérait la voix féminine comme plus agile que la masculine, mais qu'il attendait aussi plus d'agilité des femmes instrumentistes, à en juger par le n° [29]. Comme le but de ces vocalises était dès le départ d'ordre pratique, elles sont classées ici progressivement par niveau de difficulté, plutôt que chronologiquement. Malgré leurs humbles intentions avouées, beaucoup d'entre elles révèlent chez Fauré une inspiration qui prend soudain son envol (en particulier à partir du n° [20]), à la hauteur de ses meilleures mélodies.

Exceptionnellement, le n° [28] fut composé pour publication, dans un recueil de *Vocalises-Études* réunies, peut-être à l'instigation de Fauré, par Amédée-Louis Hettich, professeur de chant[3]. Pour son manuel, Hettich commanda des pièces à plusieurs compositeurs, dont Dukas, d'Indy, Hahn, Koechlin, Ravel et Ropartz ; la contribution de Fauré ouvre le premier volume, publié au début de 1907. La date similaire du présent n° [29], ajoutée à d'autres aspects de sa présentation manuscrite, laisse à penser que cette extraordinaire cantilène pourrait également avoir été conçue pour le recueil de Hettich, mais jugée trop difficile – et imposée plutôt aux élèves du Conservatoire les plus à même d'y survivre ! Cette vocalise se détache de toute l'œuvre de Fauré, révélant combien il était profondément versé dans l'art de J. S. Bach.

Il était d'usage pour les professeurs du Conservatoire de se partager la composition des morceaux d'examens d'une année donnée. Au cours de sa période de directeur, Fauré – qui auparavant avait écrit des épreuves de déchiffrage respectivement pour violoncelle, flûte, piano, violon et harpe[4] – se concentra sur les morceaux de déchiffrage vocal, confiant la tâche à des collègues quand son emploi du temps était trop occupé par des concerts ou des projets de composition majeurs. La collection de vocalises d'examen qui subsiste révèle des contrastes stylistiques prononcés au sein des contributions des différents compositeurs, mais ceux-ci sont encore plus marqués entre celles de Fauré et toutes les autres[5]. Les vocalises de Fauré commencent toujours plus simplement, en faisant en général chanter au candidat un accord parfait, et évitent les roulades opératiques, les clichés et les figurations pianistiques gênantes : elles sondent tranquillement, mais sûrement (et parfois malicieusement), les compétences vocales et musicales du candidat.

Les appendices

Ces qualités sont d'une importance cruciale pour un groupe de seize vocalises du Conservatoire datant des années 1910-1915, dont il ne subsiste que des copies officielles omettant le nom du compositeur. Plusieurs facteurs incitent fortement à penser qu'elles sont aussi de Fauré, et justifient leur présence ici en tant qu'Appendice 1. Leur style est très proche de celui des vocalises authentifiées de Fauré, et éloigné de celui de tous les autres compositeurs identifiés de vocalises. Elles forment aussi le seul ensemble anonyme de vocalises, le Conservatoire ayant normalement conservé les manuscrits originaux des autres compositeurs (qui, à la différence de celles de Fauré, sont généralement signées par leurs auteurs) et les ayant identifiés sur des copies manuscrites. De tels manquements apparents au protocole s'expliqueraient le plus naturellement si l'auteur des pièces non attribuées était le directeur de l'institution. Les pièces en question étant essentiellement plus courtes et plus simples, les autographes, sans doute notés sur des morceaux épars de papier à musique, pourraient avoir été perdus ou même jetés après la copie. Plusieurs de ces pièces révèlent des traits caractéristiques de Fauré, telles les surprises tonales ou les marches au milieu des n[os] [ii], [x] et [xi] ; les soudains bonds d'octave à la fin d'une pièce (comme dans plusieurs des vocalises authentifiées de Fauré) ; ou les cadences évitées, ou piégées d'une autre manière, qui peuvent facilement désarçonner le chanteur inattentif – notamment dans les dernières mesures du n[o] [xvi]. La gamme montante à partir de la tonique qui ouvre les n[os] [iv], [vii] et [xii] est également une tactique tout à fait caractéristique de Fauré (voir, par exemple, n[o] [28]). Ces vocalises sont elles aussi classées par ordre de difficulté technique pour servir aux mêmes fins que le groupe principal. L'Appendice 2 reproduit les dictées musicales conçues par Fauré en 1907 et 1909, qui peuvent être utiles comme exercices vocaux non accompagnés.

Caractéristiques musicales

Comme nous l'avons noté, les vocalises de Fauré mettent tranquillement à l'épreuve et développent à la fois la musicalité et la technique vocale, de manière plus précise que les exercices fleuris devenus depuis longtemps la norme. Commençant généralement par des notes de l'accord parfait à découvert, elles explorent ensuite des éléments essentiels comme la maîtrise de la respiration, la pureté de timbre et la stabilité des hauteurs et des rythmes, parfois sur de gênantes inflexions modales dans l'accompagnement. Les accompagnements de clavier, de texture simple, obligent les chanteurs à trouver leur chemin d'une note à l'autre le plus souvent sans l'aide de figurations directrices, avec des intervalles vocaux de plus en plus délicats et des progressions mélodiques peu intuitives à maîtriser. Sans indication de phrasé dans la plupart des manuscrits, les élèves chanteurs qui déchiffraient devaient utiliser leur intelligence et lire en avance pour jauger et modeler la longueur des phrases, en particulier quand Fauré prolonge une mélodie ou la transpose soudain d'une octave, alors qu'elle semble sur le point de se détendre à une cadence. Les obstacles enharmoniques sont dans le même esprit, tel le *mi*♭ lié à un *ré*♯ dans le n[o] [25] (piège que Fauré pose aussi dans des épreuves de déchiffrage instrumental). Cette vocalise particulière incarne le penchant de Fauré pour le jeu tonal et enharmonique, ses quatre premières mesures passant de *la*♭ à *ut*♭ majeur et revenant (tel le premier geste harmonique de *La Bonne Chanson*), avant que l'harmonie de septième sur *si* à la mesure 7 ne joue enharmoniquement sur le *do*♭ de la mesure 3[6].

Si les vocalises écrites pour le Conservatoire par d'autres compositeurs imitent pour l'essentiel l'air de *bel canto*, celles de Fauré ressemblent beaucoup plus à des mélodies, avec des gestes ou des tours de phrase fauréens caractéristiques, même dans les plus simples, outre certains échos plus francs comme ceux de *Lydia* dans le n[o] [20]. Tout cela complète et étaie son introduction de la mélodie comme élément fondamental dans l'enseignement du chant au Conservatoire. Dans une lettre écrite peu de temps avant son départ à la retraite, Fauré réaffirmait que ses réformes de l'enseignement du chant étaient parmi les plus réalisations dont il était le plus fier en tant que directeur, soulignant la place accordée à la formation technique et l'importance du solfège[7]. Les défis posés par ses vocalises sont aussi puissants et essentiels pour les chanteurs d'aujourd'hui qu'ils l'étaient il y a un siècle.

Suggestions d'interprétation

Les vocalises de Fauré ont deux fonctions importantes. Dans leur forme originale d'épreuves de déchiffrage vocal, elles exigent et développent une conscience auditive aiguë, le placement de la voix et la vigilance musicale. Une étude plus approfondie peut instiller et améliorer la justesse d'intonation, la pureté de timbre, l'articulation et la maîtrise du souffle, tandis que les audaces tonales des pièces, leur lignes mélodiques souples et leur phrasé fluide en font une préparation idéale pour la mélodie en général, et la mélodie française en particulier.

On ne sait pas exactement comment Fauré ou les examinateurs du Conservatoire voulaient qu'elles soient chantées. Au moins certaines d'entre elles pourraient avoir été solfiées à la manière traditionnelle française, mais cela n'aurait guère été possible pour les plus avancées (notamment le n[o] [29]) ; peut-être seulement certaines des plus simples étaient-elles destinées à être solfiées, suivant des directives données sur le moment. Les indications les plus utiles à cet égard proviennent de la « Petite préface » de Hettich au volume de *Vocalises-Études* qui s'ouvre sur la contribution de Fauré (le présent n[o] [28]) :

> Ces vocalises seront généralement chantées sur la voyelle *A* : mais tous ceux qui pratiquent le chant, enseignants et enseignés, savent que l'*A* dans la voix est aussi multiple que le vert dans la campagne ou le bleu dans le ciel. Selon l'organe et selon les registres, l'*A* revêtant l'accent circonflexe ou l'accent grave devra donc se teinter d'*O* ou d'*E*. Il sera même utile de recourir franchement à ces voyelles et de les employer conjointement avec l'*A* dans le cours d'une même vocalise. L'*É* fortement dental, variant de l'*E*, corrigera efficacement l'émission gutturale ou sourde.
>
> Pour procéder graduellement à la tension et au rapprochement des cordes ainsi que l'exige la physiologie laryngée, il est souvent utile et toujours prudent de faire précéder la voyelle d'émission d'une des consonnes explosives : *M-B-P* ; chacune de ces consonnes correspondant aux degrés d'intensité : *piano*, *mezzoforte*, *forte*. Les voix gutturales ou sourdes emploieront le *V* qui leur assure le précieux concours des dents et des lèvres.

Outre le travail avec différentes voyelles et consonnes, les interprètes pourront souhaiter expérimenter avec différents phrasés, modelés et couleurs dynamiques. Le phrasé marqué par Fauré dans les n[os] [20] et [28] a été pris ici comme modèle pour l'ajout de respirations aux autres vocalises. Celles-ci doivent être considérées comme des suggestions, et uniquement en cas de besoin lorsqu'elles sont entre parenthèses. On peut travailler les vocalises sans indication de tempo à différents tempi (ce qui peut du reste s'appliquer à toutes), en progressant doucement vers un tempo coulant (souvent assez agile) sans sacrifier la régularité du tempo ni l'exactitude du rythme et des hauteurs. Fauré était réputé pour être sourcilleux sur ces questions ; il tenait à ce qu'on reste en mesure, ce qu'il contrebalançait par le rejet de toute lourdeur dans le tempo et une forte aversion à l'encontre de tout effet de pâmoison ou de retard sentimental.

Étant donné les défis divers que posent ces pièces, on pourra évidemment débattre de l'ordre exact de difficulté technique. Certaines progressions claires sont cependant évidentes (indépendamment de la chronologie des pièces), par exemple dans les figurations séquentielles des n[os] [7–9], et plus généralement dans leurs exigences sans cesse croissantes d'agilité vocale et rythmique, dans les intervalles contrastés ou inattendus, dans le maintien de la justesse de l'intonation face aux imprévisibles inflexions tonales de l'accompagnement. (À partir du n° [25], on trouvera quelques épreuves extrêmement redoutables à cet égard.) À des fins pratiques, un résumé des difficultés perçues dans les vocalises est donné ici page XIV.

Note de l'éditeur

Les manuscrits des vocalises de Fauré nous offrent un aperçu rare sur sa carrière active. N'ayant jamais été préparés pour publication, les vingt-huit autographes du Conservatoire qui subsistent semblent des brouillons de travail finaux qui serviraient aussi de copies au net. Les moins difficiles et les plus courtes furent probablement expédiées pendant des semaines très actives au bureau ; certaines suggèrent une soudaine inspiration qui aurait surpris Fauré, tandis que d'autres témoignent d'une réflexion et d'une préparation considérables, développant peut-être une conception musicale à partir d'une réserve de matériau existant. (Quelques-unes sont écrites au verso de pages de brouillon pour des œuvres comme le Cinquième Impromptu et *Pénélope*.) Les passages retravaillés visibles sur plusieurs manuscrits témoignent du soin que Fauré leur accorda. En particulier, la section conclusive du n° [29] montre une révision qui visait probablement à clarifier la continuité de la ligne ; malgré tout, la version plus ancienne du passage est si remarquable (et utile sur le plan vocal) qu'elle est également imprimée ici.

Les indications de tempo n'apparaissent que lorsqu'elles figurent dans les sources. Les difficultés rythmiques inhabituelles du n° [29] ont justifié exceptionnellement une indication métronomique de l'éditeur. Tous les indications entre crochets sont de l'éditeur ; les altérations de précaution entre parenthèses apparaissent ainsi dans les sources. Les liaisons de prolongation et de phrasé de l'éditeur sont en pointillé. Tous les phrasés sont de l'éditeur à l'exception de ceux des n[os] [20] et [28].

Remerciements

Les éditeurs souhaitent remercier chaleureusement tous ceux qui ont aidé à la préparation de la présente édition : Mme Yvette Isselin des Archives nationales de France ; Mmes Anne Bongrain, Bérengère de l'Epine et Marie-Hélène Coudroy-Saghaï du Conservatoire de Paris ; Mme Dominique Hausfater et M. Yann Mével de la Médiathèque Hector Berlioz du Conservatoire ; le personnel du département de musique à la Bibliothèque nationale de France à Paris ; et les nombreux collègues interprètes et enseignants qui leur ont apporté leur soutien enthousiaste, leur expertise et leurs précieuses remarques musicales. Les éditeurs remercient également le Arts and Humanities Research Council (R.U.), qui a soutenu les recherches pour la présente édition par l'intermédiaire de la Royal Academy of Music de Londres.

London, 2013 *Roy Howat & Emily Kilpatrick*
(Traduction: Dennis Collins)

---

[1] Lettre du 5 novembre 1905, Étienne Dujardin-Beaumetz (sous-secrétaire d'État des Beaux-Arts) à Fauré, comprenant une directive du ministère de l'Éducation et des Beaux-Arts dont la formulation fut très probablement inspirée par Fauré lui-même ; Archives nationales de France, AJ^{37} 84/6. La directive spécifie que la première année d'études vocales au Conservatoire doit être consacrée presque exclusivement au travail des exercices et des vocalises. Pour les transcriptions complètes des documents officiels relatifs aux réformes de Fauré, et sur les détails des procédures d'examen au Conservatoire, voir Anne Bongrain, *Le Conservatoire National de Musique et de Déclamation 1900–1930: Documents historiques et administratifs*, Paris, 2012, p. 17–23, 41, 75–77 et 84–87.

[2] Les variations dans le niveau technique reflètent aussi le fait que les vocalises ont été conçues pour différents examens au cours de l'année d'études au Conservatoire (sans que cela permette de les classer de manière cohérente ; les épreuves existantes étaient parfois réutilisées pour des examens différents dans les années suivantes). Les examens habituels étaient l'admission (octobre/novembre), les examens en cours d'année, en janvier/février et en mai, et le concours de fin d'année en juin/juillet.

[3] *Répertoire Moderne de Vocalises-Etudes*, publiées sous la direction de A. L. Hettich, professeur au Conservatoire (Paris, Éditions Alphonse Leduc, 1907–) ; prévue à l'origine en trois volumes, la série comportait sept gros volumes (cinquante-six cahiers) au moment de la mort de Hettich en 1937, avec Messiaen et Poulenc parmi les compositeurs ultérieurs.

[4] Les pièces en question pour violoncelle, flûte, piano et violon sont publiées chez Peters dans les volumes EP 7571, 7514, 7601 (comprenant les *Pièces brèves* pour piano de Fauré) et 7515.

[5] Les autres compositeurs de vocalises pour les examens du Conservatoire entre 1905 et le départ à la retraite de Fauré en 1920 comprennent Georges Caussade, Émile Pessard, Marcel Chadeigne, Henri Busser, J. Morpain, Jules Mouquet, Eugène Piffaretti, Paul Rougnon, Paul Vidal, et Jacques et Louise Samuel-Rousseau. La plupart d'entre eux participèrent également aux recueils de Hettich.

[6] Les lignes vocales de ces vocalises, pour leur usage premier lors des examens, étaient également hérissées de changements de clef, avec essentiellement différentes clefs d'ut (élément omis de la présente édition). La rigueur pédagogique de Fauré – à quoi s'ajoutait peut-être sa malice innée – est évidente dans le placement de ces changements de clef : alors que ses collègues tendaient à les mettre après des fins de phrase, pour aider les candidats, Fauré les place souvent en milieu de phrase et entre des intervalles délicats. Ce n'est pas pour rien que l'un de ses surnoms au Conservatoire était « Robespierre ».

[7] Lettre à Paul Léon, 26 décembre 1919, citée dans Jean-Michel Nectoux, « Gabriel Fauré au Conservatoire de Paris : une philosophie pour l'enseignement », in *Le Conservatoire de Paris : Des Menus-Plaisirs à la Cité de la musique, 1795–1995*, éd. Anne Bongrain et Yves Gérard (Paris : Éditions Buchet/Chastel, 1996), p. 221.

Vorwort

Als Gabriel Fauré 1905 zum Direktor des Pariser Konservatoriums ernannt wurde, war es eines seiner wichtigsten Anliegen – und ersten Errungenschaften –, die Gesangspädagogik vollständig zu reformieren. Dass die Lehre seit langem bis zur Besessenheit von der zweitklassigen Grand opéra (Auber, Halévy und dergleichen) geprägt war, veranlasste ihn, den Gesangsunterricht ganz und gar neu auszurichten und das Pflichtstudium des Kunstliedes sowie „grundlegende Stimmbildungsübungen für eine flexible Stimme, für den Ansatz der Stimme, für Artikulation und Klangerzeugung" einzuführen.[1] Zu diesem Zweck komponierte er zwischen 1906 und 1916 zahlreiche Vokalisen mit Instrumentalbegleitung, die dem Konservatorium für die Prüfungen im Blattsingen dienten. Ein Jahrhundert lang blieben diese Vokalisen, die sich heute im Besitz der Archives nationales de France befinden, der musikalischen Welt vorenthalten. Die vorliegende Erstveröffentlichung ist von herausragender Bedeutung für die Unterrichtsliteratur im Bereich Gesang. Sie ist eine wunderbare Quelle kunstvoll gestalteter, mitunter bezaubernder Gesangsübungen für Anfänger bis Fortgeschrittene auf virtuosem Niveau von einem der besten Liedkomponisten der Geschichte.

Da Fauré bezüglich seines eigenen Schaffens stets bescheiden war, hatte er nie geplant, seine für das Konservatorium komponierten Vokalisen zu veröffentlichen. Stücke unterschiedlichen technischen Schwierigkeitsgrades folgen in chronologischer Reihenfolge unvorhergesehen aufeinander, was vermutlich das sich von Jahr zu Jahr ändernde, heterogene Niveau der Studenten widerspiegelt.[2] Studenten und Studentinnen wurden zu dieser Zeit unterschiedlich geprüft (so auch Sänger und Instrumentalisten). Die für jede Kategorie individuell komponierten Vokalisen legen zum Großteil nahe, dass Fauré die weibliche Stimme für beweglicher erachtete als die männliche; den Instrumentalisten wiederum verlangte er – Nr. [29] nach zu urteilen – noch mehr Beweglichkeit ab. Da Fauré mit diesen Vokalisen grundsätzlich einen praktischen Zweck verfolgte und auch die vorliegende Ausgabe einen solchen beabsichtigt, sind die Stücke hier nach steigendem Schwierigkeitsgrad und nicht chronologisch geordnet. Trotz ihres vorgeblich bescheidenen Zwecks zeichnen sich viele dieser Übungen durch inspirierte Eingebungen aus (besonders ab Nr. [20]), wodurch einige von ihnen auf einer Stufe mit den besten Liedkompositionen Faurés stehen.

Nur die Nr. [28] wurde als einziges Stück für die Veröffentlichung komponiert und erschien in der von dem Gesangslehrer Amédée-Louis Hettich – vermutlich auf Betreiben Faurés – vorgelegten Sammlung *Vocalises Études*.[3] Für dieses Kompendium gab Hettich Kompositionen bei Dukas, d'Indy, Hahn, Koechlin, Ravel und Ropartz in Auftrag. Faurés Beitrag eröffnet den ersten Band, der Anfang 1907 publiziert wurde. Die ähnlich datierte Nr. [29] dieser Ausgabe legt aufgrund weiterer formaler Aspekte der Handschrift nahe, dass diese außergewöhnliche Kantilene möglicherweise auch für Hettichs Sammlung konzipiert war, sich jedoch als zu schwierig erwies – und stattdessen den Prüflingen des Konservatoriums untergeschoben wurde, die sich dabei am ehesten behaupten würden. Diese Vokalise ragt aus Faurés gesamtem Schaffen heraus und zeugt davon, wie sehr er von der Kunst J. S. Bachs durchdrungen war.

Für Professoren des Konservatoriums war es üblich, dass sich jeder an der Komposition von Prüfungsstücken für sämtliche Jahrgänge beteiligte. Während seines Direktorats konzentrierte sich Fauré – der in früheren Jahren Blattspiel-Prüfungsstücke für Cello, Flöte, Klavier, Violine und Harfe beigetragen hatte[4] – auf Blattsingprüfungen und betraute einen Kollegen mit der Aufgabe, wenn er durch Konzerte oder größere Kompositionsvorhaben ausgelastet war. Die erhalten gebliebene Sammlung von Prüfungs-Vokalisen lässt ausgeprägte stilistische Unterschiede zwischen den Stücken verschiedener Komponisten erkennen, vor allem aber zwischen denen Faurés und allen anderen.[5] Faurés Vokalkompositionen beginnen grundsätzlich einfacher, gewöhnlich mit einem Dreiklang, und vermeiden die üblichen opernartigen Rouladen, Klischees und ablenkenden Klavier-Figurationen. Im Verlauf eines Stückes werden langsam, aber sicher (und manchmal mit hintergründigem Schalk) die gesanglichen und musikalischen Fähigkeiten des Kandidaten auf die Probe gestellt.

DIE APPENDIZES

Die oben genannten Eigenschaften treffen auf entscheidende Weise auch auf sechzehn für das Konservatorium verfasste, zusammengehörige Vokalisen aus den Jahren 1910–15 zu. Sie sind lediglich in Form von offiziellen Abschriften des Conservertoires erhalten, in denen der Komponist nicht genannt wird. Mehrere Faktoren weisen deutlich darauf hin, dass auch diese Stücke von Fauré stammen und sprechen dafür, sie der vorliegenden Ausgabe als Appendix 1 beizufügen. Stilistisch ähneln sie deutlich den authentifizierten Vokalisen Faurés und keineswegs den Kompositionen eines der anderen namentlich identifizierten Autoren. Es sind zudem die einzigen Vokalisen ohne Angabe der Urheberschaft, während das Konservatorium üblicherweise die Originalhandschriften anderer Beiträger aufbewahrte (diese wurden im Gegensatz zu Faurés Kompositionen für gewöhnlich vom Autor signiert) und auf Abschriften die Urheber identifizierte. Solcherlei offensichtliche Protokollverstöße lassen sich am plausibelsten dadurch erklären, dass es sich beim Autor der anonymen Stücke um den Direktor der Institution selbst handelte. Die Autographen der betroffenen, meist kürzeren und einfacheren Stücke, die wahrscheinlich auf Notenpapierresten verfasst wurden, sind womöglich verschollen oder wurden nach Abschrift vernichtet. Mehrere dieser Vokalisen weisen eindeutige Stilmerkmale Faurés auf, darunter unerwartete Modulationen oder Sequenzen in der Stückmitte der Nrn. [ii], [x] und [xi], plötzliche Oktavsprünge am Ende eines Stückes (wie in einigen authentifizierten Vokalisen Faurés) oder strategisch platzierte Trugschlüsse oder auf andere Weise mit einer Falle versehene Kadenzen, die den unaufmerksamen Sänger leicht ins Schleudern bringen können (so z. B. in den Schlusstakten der Nr. [xvi]). Auch die von der Tonika aufsteigende Tonleiter zu Beginn der Nrn. [iv], [vii] und [xii] ist ein für Fauré äußerst charakteristisches Merkmal (vgl. z. B. Nr. [28]). Die in Appendix 1 enthaltenen Vokalisen sind vor dem selben Hintergrund wie die Stücke im Hauptteil dieser Ausgabe nach ansteigendem technischen Schwierigkeitsgrad geordnet. Appendix 2 bildet Notendiktatprüfungen ab, die Fauré zwischen 1907 und 1909 verfasste. Sie können als unbegleitete Gesangsübungen dienen.

Musikalische Besonderheiten

Gezielter als die überladenen Übungen, die lange Zeit als Norm galten, testen und entwickeln Faurés Vokalisen Schritt für Schritt die musikalischen und gesanglichen Fähigkeiten des Kandidaten. Sie beginnen für gewöhnlich mit gebrochenen Dreiklängen, prüfen dann Grundlagen wie Atemtechnik, Klangreinheit sowie durchgängige Tonhöhensicherheit und rhythmische Präzision, während die Begleitung teils irritierende harmonische Rückungen vollzieht. Angesichts der strukturell einfachen Klavierbegleitung muss der Sänger von Ton zu Ton finden, ohne sich dabei auf richtungweisende Figurationen stützen zu können. Die zu singenden Intervalle werden zunehmend komplizierter, auch nicht intuitiv fortschreitende Melodien müssen bewältigt werden. Da Phrasen meist nicht kenntlich gemacht waren, hatten die Studenten während des Blattsingens ihren Verstand zu benutzen und vorausschauend zu lesen, um sie entsprechend ihrer Länge zu beurteilen und zu gestalten. Dies trifft insbesondere auf Passagen zu, in denen Fauré eine Melodie ausdehnt oder sie plötzlich um eine Oktave transponiert, wo sie sich doch in eine einfache Kadenz zu begeben schien. Ähnlicher Natur sind Gefahren enharmonischer Verwechslung, wie das an das *Es* gebundene *Dis* in Nr. [25] (eine Falle, die Fauré auch Instrumentalisten in Blattspielprüfungen stellte). Diese konkrete Vokalise verkörpert Faurés Vorliebe für modale und tonale Mehrdeutigkeit: Die ersten vier Takte pendeln von As- nach Ces-Dur und zurück (wie der erste Harmoniewechsel in *La Bonne Chanson*), ehe in Takt 7 ein H^7-Akkord erscheint und Fauré mit einer enharmonischen Verwechslung zum noch in Takt 3 verwendeten Ces-Dur spielt.[6]

Während für das Konservatorium geschriebene Vokalisen anderer Komponisten meist die Belcanto-Arie nachahmen, klingen jene von Fauré mehr wie *Mélodies*, und selbst in den einfachsten Stücken finden sich ausgesprochen Fauré-typische Gesten oder musikalische Wendungen. Offenkundigere Liedanklänge, wie beispielsweise an *Lydia*, treten in Nr. [20] zutage. Dies veranschaulicht Faurés Entscheidung, das Kunstlied zum elementaren Bestandteil des konservatorischen Gesangscurriculums zu machen. In einem Brief, den er kurz vor seinem Eintritt in den Ruhestand verfasste, beteuert er, dass die Reformen der Gesangspädagogik zu denjenigen Errungenschaften als Direktor zählen, auf die er am meisten stolz sei und stellt die Bedeutung der technischen Ausbildung und des Solfège heraus.[7] Seine gesammelten Vokalisen stellen auch heute genauso wirksame und entscheidende gesangliche Herausforderungen wie noch vor einem Jahrhundert.

Anregungen zur Ausführung

Faurés Vokalisen dienen zwei wichtigen Zielen. In ihrer ursprünglichen Gestalt als Blattsingprüfungen erfordern und entwickeln sie ein feines Gehör, einen guten Stimmansatz und musikalische Aufmerksamkeit. Ein vertieftes Studium lehrt und fördert die genaue Intonation, Klangreinheit, Artikulation und Atemkontrolle, während die Stücke aufgrund ihrer zum Teil gewagten Modulationen, geschmeidigen Melodielinien und fließenden Phrasierungen als ideale Vorbereitung auf das Kunstlied im Allgemeinen und insbesondere auf dessen französische Spielart *Mélodie* dienen können.

Welche konkrete Vokalisierung Fauré und den Prüfern des Konservatoriums vorschwebte, bleibt offen. Zumindest manche Stücke wurden möglicherweise in der traditionellen französischen Art solfeggiert, bei den komplizierteren ist dies jedoch kaum möglich (insbesondere Nr. [29]). Vielleicht sollten nur einige der einfacheren Stücke in bestimmten Situationen solfeggiert werden. Die in diesem Zusammenhang aufschlussreichsten Hinweise stammen aus dem „Petite préface", das Hettich seinen gesammelten, mit einem Beitrag von Fauré (hier Nr. [28]) eröffneten *Vocalises-Études* voranstellte:

> Diese Vokalisen werden gewöhnlich auf dem Vokal *A* gesungen: Doch all diejenigen, die sich mit Gesang befassen, ob Lehrer oder Schüler, wissen, dass das klingende *A* so vielfältig sein kann wie das Grün der Landschaft und das Blau des Himmels. Je nach Stimme und Register kann das *A* mit accent circonflexe oder grave gebildet werden und somit in die Nähe von *O* oder *E* rücken. Es wird sich, offen gesagt, sogar als nützlich erweisen, diese Vokale innerhalb einer Vokalise mit *A* zu kombinieren. Das stark dentale *E*, eine Variante des normalen *E*, korrigiert auf effiziente Weise einen kehligen oder gedämpften Klang.
>
> [...] Um nach und nach eine Spannung und Annäherung der Stimmbänder zu erzielen – wie es die Physiologie des Kehlkopfes erfordert –, ist es häufig nützlich und vernünftig, dem Vokal einen plosiven Konsonanten voranzustellen: *M–B–P*, mit entsprechend dynamischer Steigerung *p–mf–f*. Sänger mit kehliger oder leiser Stimme können das *V* verwenden, wodurch die notwendige Beteiligung von Zähnen und Lippen sichergestellt wird.

Neben dem Üben verschiedener Vokal- und Konsonantklänge kann auch mit Phraseneinteilung und -gestaltung sowie dynamischer Schattierung experimentiert werden. Die von Fauré in Nr. [20] und [28] kenntlich gemachten Phrasen dienten als Vorlage für die Atemzeichen, die den übrigen Vokalisen redaktionell hinzugefügt wurden. Diese sollten als Vorschläge betrachtet werden. Atemzeichen in runden Klammern sind lediglich für den Bedarfsfall vermerkt. Vokalisen ohne Tempovorschrift können in unterschiedlichen Tempi ausgeführt werden (dies gilt in der Tat auch für andere Vokalisen), wobei sich der Sänger gemächlich auf ein schnelleres (manchmal recht flinkes) Tempo steigert, ohne dabei an Tempo- und Rhythmusfestigkeit oder Tonhöhensicherheit einzubüßen. Fauré war in diesen Aspekten bekanntermaßen pedantisch. Während er höchsten Wert auf die Einhaltung des Tempos legte, verabscheute er schwerfällige Tempi und jede Art schwindender Effekte und sentimentalen Verweilens.

Aufgrund der vielfältigen Herausforderungen dieser Stücke ist deren Anordnung nach technischem Schwierigkeitsgrad weiterhin diskutierbar. Offenkundig ist jedoch der wachsende Anspruch, unabhängig von der Chronologie der Stücke, etwa durch figurative Sequenzen in den Nrn. [7–9] und, allgemeiner gesagt, durch stetig steigende Anforderungen an die vokale und rhythmische Behändigkeit, die Bewältigung kontrastierender oder unerwarteter Intervalle oder die Tonhöhensicherheit trotz unvorhersehbarer Modulationen in der Begleitstimme (ab Nr. [25] kommen stark modulierende Passagen auf den Sänger zu). Zur Orientierung wurde von den Herausgebern eine Auflistung der Stücke gemäß ihren Anforderungen vorangestellt (siehe S. XIV).

Anmerkungen der Herausgeber

Die Handschriften der Vokalisen Faurés bieten einen seltenen Einblick in dessen erfülltes Berufsleben. Die achtundzwanzig erhaltenen, nicht zur Veröffentlichung vorgesehenen Autographe des Konservatoriums scheinen endgültige Arbeitsentwürfe zu sein, die auch als Reinschriften verwendet wurden. Die unkomplizierteren und kürzeren Stücke schrieb Fauré wahrscheinlich während arbeitsintensiver Wochen schnell im Büro nieder. Bei anderen gab es momentane Inspirationen, und wieder andere lassen reifliche Überlegung und Vorbereitung erkennen, ein musikalisches Konzept aus möglicherweise bereits bestehendem Material zu entwickeln. (Einige Stücke wurden auf Rückseiten von Entwürfen, wie etwa für das Fünfte Impromptu und *Pénélope*, verfasst.) Die auf vielen Handschriften erkennbaren Überarbeitungen bezeugen die Sorgfalt, mit der Fauré dabei vorging. Besonders der Schlussteil von Nr. [29] zeigt eine Revision, durch die das Stück vermutlich eine klare, fortlaufende Linie erhalten sollte. Dennoch ist Faurés frühere Lesart der Passage so bemerkenswert (und gesanglich wertvoll), dass sie in der vorliegenden Ausgabe abgedruckt wurde.

Tempovorschriften stehen nur, insofern die Quellen darüber Auskunft geben. Eine Ausnahme bildet Nr. [29], deren außergewöhnliche rhythmische Anforderungen die Herausgeber veranlasst haben, ein Metrum zu empfehlen. Bei Angaben in eckigen Klammern handelt es sich um redaktionelle Ergänzungen, Warnungsakzidenzien in runden Klammern hingegen wurden den Quellen entnommen. Redaktionelle Binde- und Haltebögen sind durch Strichelung gekennzeichnet. Alle Phrasen wurden seitens der Herausgeber gegliedert, ausgenommen jene in Nr. [20] und [28].

Danksagungen

Die Herausgeber danken herzlich all jenen, die bei der Erstellung der vorliegenden Ausgabe geholfen haben: Mme Yvette Isselin (Archives nationales de France), Mmes Anne Bongrain, Bérengère de l'Epine und Marie-Hélène Coudroy-Saghaï (Conservatoire de Paris), Mme Dominique Hausfater und M. Yann Mével (Médiathèque Hector Berlioz am Conservatoire), den Mitarbeitern der Bibliothèque nationale de France in Paris sowie den zahlreichen Musiker- und Lehrerkollegen für die unschätzbaren Hinweise und Anregungen. Dank gebührt auch dem Arts and Humanities Research Council (UK) und der Royal Academy of Music, London, für die Unterstützung der Forschungsarbeit zur vorliegenden Edition.

London, 2013
Roy Howat & Emily Kilpatrick
(Übersetzung: Lore Horlamus)

---

[1] Brief vom 5. November 1905, Étienne Dujardin-Beaumetz (Unterstaatssekretär für Schöne Künste) an Fauré, mit einer Richtlinie des Ministeriums für Bildung und Kunst, deren Wortlaut mit großer Wahrscheinlichkeit von Fauré selbst angeregt wurde; Archives nationales de France, AJ^{37} 84/6. Die Richtlinie legt fest, dass das erste Jahr der Gesangsausbildung am Konservatorium fast ausschließlich dem Studium von Übungen und Vokalisen gewidmet sein soll. Vollständige Wiedergabe der amtlichen Unterlagen zu Faurés Reformen sowie Details zu den Prüfungsverfahren am Konservatorium bei Anne Bongrain, *Le Conservatoire National de Musique et de Déclamation 1900–1930: Documents historiques et administratifs*, Paris 2012, S. 17–23, 41, 75–77 und 84–87.

[2] Die unterschiedlichen technischen Anforderungen der Vokalisen spiegeln zudem wider, dass sie für über das Jahr verteilte verschiedene Prüfungen des Konservatoriums konzipiert waren (auch wenn dies keine konsistente Bewertung zulässt und bestehende Tests mitunter für andere Prüfungen in späteren Jahren verwendet wurden). Die Aufnahmeprüfungen erfolgten zu Beginn des Studienjahres (Oktober/November), Trimesterprüfungen im Januar/Februar und Mai und der Jahresabschluss-Wettbewerb (*concours*) im Juni/Juli.

[3] *Répertoire Moderne de Vocalises-Etudes*, publiées sous la direction de A. L. Hettich, Professeur au Conservatoire (Paris, Editions Alphonse Leduc, 1907–); ursprünglich als dreibändige Reihe geplant, umfasste die Sammlung mit dem Tode Hettichs 1937 sieben große Bände (56 Faszikel), deren spätere Beiträge unter anderem von Messiaen und Poulenc stammen.

[4] Die entsprechenden Blattspiel-Stücke für Cello, Flöte, Klavier und Violine sind in der Edition Peters unter EP 7571, 7514, 7601 (enthält Faurés *Pièces brèves* für Klavier) und 7515 erschienen.

[5] Zu den weiteren Komponisten der zwischen 1905 und Faurés Pensionierung im Jahr 1920 verfassten Stücke für die Blattsingprüfungen des Konservatoriums zählten Georges Caussade, Émile Pessard, Marcel Chadeigne, Henri Busser, J. Morpain, Jules Mouquet, Eugène Piffaretti, Paul Rougnon, Paul Vidal und Jacques und Louise Samuel-Rousseau. Die meisten von ihnen trugen ebenfalls zu Hettichs Kompendium bei.

[6] Die Gesangsstimmen dieser Vokalisen beinhalteten zwecks ihrer ursprünglichen Verwendung in Prüfungen außerdem erschwerende Notenschlüsselwechsel, so vor allem bewegliche C-Schlüssel (in der vorliegenden Ausgabe nicht übernommen). Faurés pädagogische Strenge, die er neben seiner angeborenen Verschmitztheit besaß, wird in der Platzierung dieser Schlüsselwechsel deutlich: Während Kollegen sie üblicherweise zuvorkommend am Beginn einer neuen Phrase vermerken, ändert Fauré den Schlüssel sehr oft in der Mitte einer Phrase und inmitten komplizierter Intervalle. Nicht ohne Grund zählte „Robespierre" zu einem seiner Spitznamen am Konservatorium.

[7] Brief an Paul Léon, 26. Dezember 1919, zitiert nach Jean-Michel Nectoux, „Gabriel Fauré au Conservatoire de Paris: Une philosophie pour l'enseignement", in *Le Conservatoire de Paris: Des Menus-Plaisirs à la Cité de la musique, 1795–1995*, hrsg. v. Anne Bongrain und Yves Gérard (Paris: Éditions Buchet/Chastel, 1996), S. 221.

Progressive technical and musical challenges posed by Fauré's vocalises

[1–3]: Accurate pitching of basic intervals and rhythms (often without help from the accompaniment); maintaining a line through deceptive or delayed cadences

[4–6]: Accurate pitching of wider and less intuitive intervals; more challenging modal shifts and cadential progressions, particularly towards the end of a piece

[7–9]: Chromatic and modal contrasts, unpredictable modulations and deceptive cadences; progressive sequential patterns

[10–12]: Vocal independence from the accompaniment, including deceptive or challenging intervals, shorter sequences and more rapid harmonic shifts; increased rhythmic flexibility (duplets alternating with triplets)

[13–16]: Precise handling of more complex rhythms and modal shifts; beauty of tone and breath control across longer, more song-like melodic lines

[17–20]: Rhythmically and melodically independent accompaniments with polyphonic imitation; increased chromaticism and modal complexity; extended scale passages, with unexpected challenges in the final bars; intensified focus on phrasing in no. [20]

[21–23]: Suppleness and nimbleness in rhythmic articulation; scales and arpeggios in increasingly virtuosic coloratura passages

[24–29]: Advanced musicianship at virtuoso level

Appendix 1:
[i–xvi]: More studies at a similar level to [1–9] above

Appendix 2: Exercises in accurate pitching and rhythm

Difficultés techniques et musicales progressives posées par les vocalises de Fauré

[1–3] : Intonation précise d'intervalles et rythmes de base (souvent sans l'aide de l'accompagnement) ; maintien d'une ligne passant par des cadences évitées ou retardées

[4–6] : Intonation précise d'intervalles plus grands et moins intuitifs ; inflexions tonales et progressions cadentielles plus difficiles, surtout vers la fin des pièces

[7–9] : Contrastes chromatiques et tonals, cadences évitées et modulations imprévisibles ; motifs séquentiels progressifs

[10–12] : Indépendance de la voix par rapport à l'accompagnement, y compris intervalles trompeurs ou difficiles, séquences plus brèves et changements harmoniques plus rapides ; flexibilité rythmique accrue (duolets alternant avec triolets)

[13–16] : Précision dans les rythmes plus complexes et les inflexions tonales ; beauté de timbre et maîtrise du souffle sur des lignes plus longues et plus chantantes

[17–20] : Accompagnements rythmiquement et mélodiquement indépendants avec imitation polyphonique ; chromatisme et complexité tonale accrus ; longs passages en gammes, avec difficultés inattendues dans les dernières mesures ; accent plus marqué sur le phrasé dans le n° [20]

[21–23] : Souplesse et agilité dans l'articulation rythmique ; gammes et arpèges dans des passages en coloratures de plus en plus virtuoses

[24–29] : Musicalité avancée au niveau virtuose

Appendice 1 :
[i–xvi] : Autres études d'un niveau similaire aux n[os] [1–9] ci-dessus

Appendice 2 : Exercices d'intonation et de rythme précis

Faurés Vokalisen nach steigendem technischem und musikalischem Schwierigkeitsgrad

[1–3]: Grundlegende Intervalle und Rhythmen präzise singen (oft ohne Hilfe der Begleitung); über Trugschlüsse oder verzögerte Kadenzen hinweg eine Linie bewahren

[4–6]: Weiter auseinanderliegende und weniger intuitive Intervalle präzise treffen; Stücke mit anspruchsvolleren Rückungen und schwerer zu folgenden tonalen Fortschreitungen, besonders gegen Ende

[7–9]: Chromatische und modale Gegenüberstellungen, unvorhersehbare Modulationen und Trugschlüsse; Sequenzketten

[10–12]: Unabhängikeit der Gesangsstimme von der Begleitung; Stücke mit trügerischen oder anspruchsvollen Intervallen, kürzeren Sequenzen und schneller aufeinanderfolgenden harmonischen Rückungen; zunehmende rhythmische Flexibilität gefordert (Duolen und Triolen im Wechsel)

[13–16]: Präzise Bewältigung komplexerer Rhythmen und Rückungen; Klangschönheit und Atemkontrolle über längere, liedhaftere Melodielinien bewahren

[17–20]: Rhythmisch und melodisch unabhängige Begleitung mit polyphoner Imitation; zunehmende Chromatik und Komplexität der Skalen; Passagen mit erweitertem Tonvorrat und unerwartete Herausforderungen in den Schlusstakten; verstärkte Fokussierung auf Phrasierung in Nr. [20]

[21–23]: Flexibilität und Behändigkeit bei der rhythmischen Artikulation; Skalen und Arpeggien in zunehmend virtuosen Koloraturpassagen

[24–29]: Fortgeschrittenes musikalisches Können auf virtuosem Niveau

Appendix 1:
[i–xvi]: Weitere Studien auf ähnlichem Niveau wie [1–9] oben

Appendix 2: Übungen zur Tonhöhensicherheit und Rhythmusfestigkeit

Contents

Key
Tonart

[1] C (1910) 2
[2] a (1913) 3
[3] C (1907) 4
[4] F (1909) 5
[5] C (1908) 6
[6] F (1913) 7
[7] C (Allegro moderato, 1908) 8
[8] G (1909) 9
[9] D (Moderato, 1914) 10
[10] C (Moderato, 1914) 11
[11] G (Allegro moderato, 1909) 12
[12] F (Allegro moderato, 1906) 13
[13] G (Andante moderato, 1906) 14
[14] F (1907) 15
[15] D (Moderato, 1915) 16
[16] D (Moderato, 1909) 17
[17] C (Andante moderato, 1907) 18
[18] F (Allegretto, 1909) 19
[19] D (Allegretto, 1908) 20
[20] F (Moderato, 1912) 21
[21] B♭ (1908) 22
[22] C (Allegretto, 1908) 23
[23] F (Moderato, 1915) 24
[24] f (Molto moderato, 1916) 25
[25] A♭ (Andante moderato, 1907) 26
[26] F (Allegro molto moderato, 1909) 27
[27] A (Moderato, 1908) 28
[28] e (Adagio, molto tranquillo) 30
[29] f (Adagio, 1907) 33

Appendix 1

[i] C (Allegro) 37
[ii] F 37
[iii] C (Allegro) 38
[iv] G 38
[v] C 39
[vi] G (Allegro, 1914) 40
[vii] C (1913) 40
[viii] G (1912) 41
[ix] C (Andante, 1911) 42
[x] G (1910) 42
[xi] F (Allegretto, 1914) 43
[xii] G (Allegretto, 1911) 44
[xiii] F (Allegretto, 1915) 45
[xiv] G (Allegretto, 1912) 46
[xv] G (Moderato, 1912) 47
[xvi] F (Moderato, 1912) 48

Appendix 2

F (Andante, 1907) 50
C (Andante, 1907) 50
A (Andantino, 1907) 50
E (Andantino, 1907) 51
D (1909) 51
C (1909) 51

Critical Commentary 52

Chronological Index of Contents 57

Vocalises

[1]

Gabriel Fauré (1845–1924)
Edited by Roy Howat and Emily Kilpatrick

Admission, 3 November 1910 (men)

[2]

Concours, 11 June 1913 (men)

4

[3]

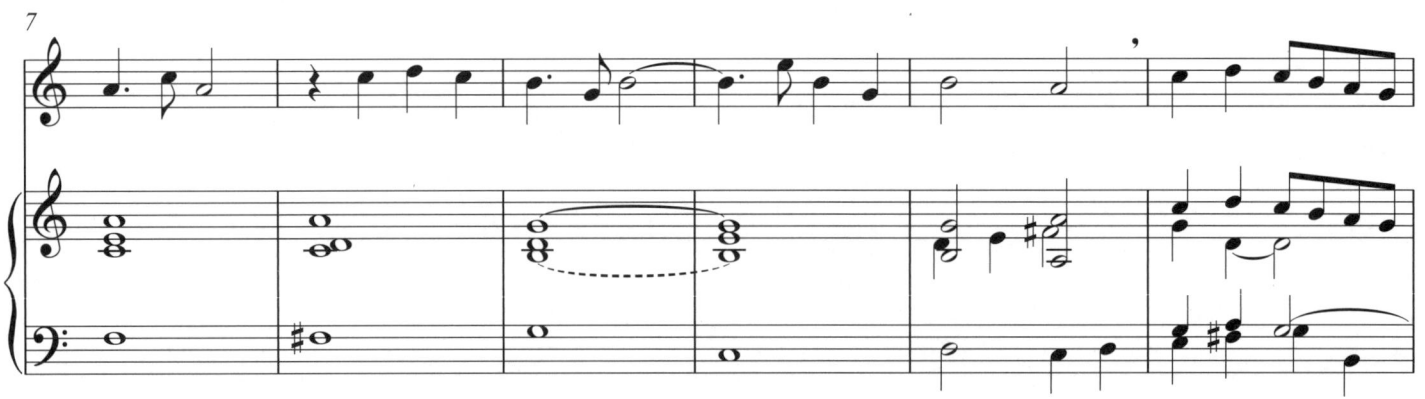

Admission, October 1907 (men)

[4]

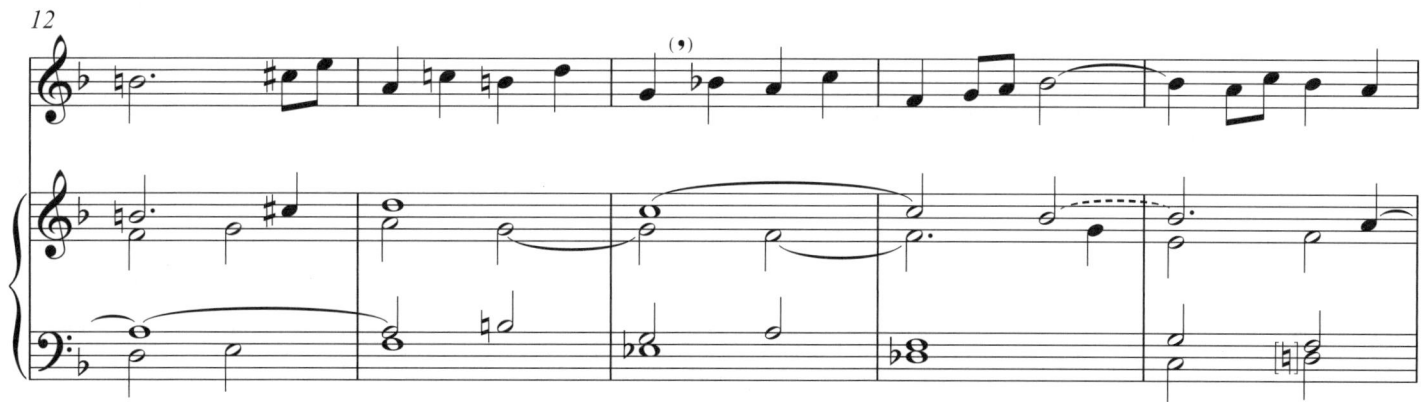

Admission, 8 November 1909 (men)

[5]

Examination, 7 January 1908 (men)

[6]

Concours, 11 June 1913 (women)

[7]

Allegro moderato

Admission, 22 October 1908 (men)

[8]

Examination, 7 January 1909 (men)

10

[9]

Examination, 5 May 1914 (women)

[10]

Examination, 5 May 1914 (men)

[11]

Admission, 9 November 1909 (women)

[12]

Examination, January 1906 (men)

14

[13]

Examination, January 1906 (women)

[14]

Admission, October 1907 (women)

16

[15]

Examination, 18 May 1915 (women and men)

[16]

Concours, 19 June 1909 (men)

[17]

Examination, May 1907 (men)

[18]

Examination, 7 January 1909 (women)

20

[19]

Concours, 13 June 1908 (men)

[20]

Concours, 12 June 1912 (women)

[21]

Examination, 7 January 1908 (women)

[22]

Admission, 23 October 1908 (women)

[23]

Concours, 16 June 1915 (women)

Molto moderato

Concours, 14 June 1916 (women and men)

26

[25]

Examination, May 1907 (women)

[26]

28

Concours, 19 June 1909 (women)

[27]

Concours, 13 June 1908 (women)

[28]

Vocalise-Étude
(published 1907)

(1) Original indication / À l'origine / Tempoangabe ursprünglich: *Andante molto moderato* (♩ = 60)

(1) Main reading as in autograph, *ossia* as in First Edition; see Critical commentary
   Version principale d'après l'autographe, *ossia* d'après la première édition; voir Commentaire critique
   Hauptlesart nach Manuskript, *ossia* nach Erstausgabe; siehe Kritischen Bericht

[29]

Adagio [♩ = c. 46–40]

Examination, May 1907 (instrumentalists' sight-singing, women)

Earlier reading:
Version primitive :
Urfassung:

Edition Peters 33415

Appendix 1

Unattributed vocalises probably by Fauré

(in technically progressive order)

Vocalises non attribuées, probablement par Fauré

(classées progressivement par niveau de difficulté)

Vokalisen, die Fauré zugeschrieben werden können

(angeordnet nach aufsteigender Schwierigkeit)

37

[i]

Admission, 21 December 1914 (men)

[ii]

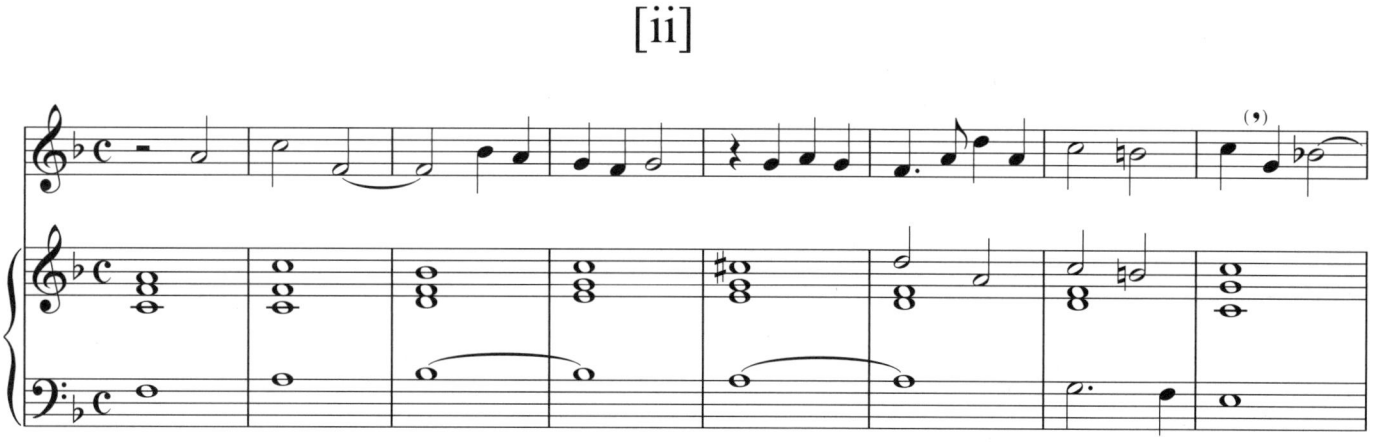

Admission, October 1913 (men)

[iii]

Examination, 2 February 1915 (men)

[iv]

Examination, 7 January 1914 (women)

[V]

Examination, 7 January 1914 (men)

40

[vi]

Concours, 4 June 1914 (men)

[vii]

Admission, October 1913 (women)

[viii]

Examination, 6 January 1912 (women)

42

[ix]

Examination, 12 January 1911 (men)

[x]

Admission, 4 November 1910 (women)

[xi]

Concours, 4 June 1914 (women)

[XII]

Examination, 12 January 1911 (women)

[XIII]

Examination, 2 February 1915 (women)

[xiv]

Concours, 12 June 1912 (men)

47

[XV]

Moderato

Examination, 8 May 1912 (men)

[XVI]

Examination, 8 May 1912 (women)

Appendix 2

Dictations

(usable as unaccompanied vocalises)

Dictations

(utilisables comme des vocalises non accompagnées)

Notendiktate

(verwendbar als Vokalisen ohne Begleitung)

Dictations

May 1907

(Singers, women)

(Singers, men)

(Instrumentalists, women)

(Instrumentalists, men)

January 1909

(Singers, women)

(Singers, men)

Critical Commentary

Editorial method

The present edition takes Fauré's autograph scores as the default source, along with the 1907 first edition of no. [28]; for Appendix 1 the official Conservatoire copies of necessity serve as default source. Any departures from or variants of these are noted. While Fauré's autographs normally convey the intrinsic polyphony of the piano lines, a few inconsistent stem notations have been adjusted, following the official copies when they clarify matters (though not when they suggest miscopying or create inconsistencies). Minor errors in the official copies are tacitly ignored.

Essential accidentals or augmentation dots are tacitly taken from any source that supplies them; similarly in the case of useful cautionary accidentals. Other redundant accidentals are omitted. Vocal lines are notated in treble clef, ignoring any clef changes in the sources, though the presence of changing clefs is noted in the source descriptions. (See Preface note 6: earlier autographs incorporate clef changes in the vocal line, later ones mostly indicate them above, the official copies working them into the vocal line.) Other aspects of editorial presentation are described in the prefatory Editorial Note.

Sources and sigla

A autograph. No duplicate autographs exist

C official Conservatoire copy, until May 1908 in an unidentified hand, thereafter probably in that of the Conservatoire copyist Louis-Jules Andrieu. Multiple copies are labelled **C1**, **C2** etc.

E printed source (no. [28] only)

The autograph of no. [28] is in the Bibliothèque nationale de France, Paris (see below). The remainder are in the Archives nationales de France, Pierrefitte-sur-Seine: shelf mark AJ^{37} 201.3 (file "Solfège de chanteurs, 1885–1925") for all except no. [29], whose shelf mark is AJ^{37} 202.1 (file "Solfège d'instrumentistes, 1885–1925"). Filed with them are the Conservatoire copies made for examinations (including those constituting Appendix 1); these include further copies made for reuse in later years and clearly derived from the existing official copies (rather than the autographs).

The autograph of no. [29] shows a presentation closer to that of no. [28]: signed and dated at the end, it is written on quality paper, suggesting it may have originated for a similar purpose (see Preface). The other Conservatoire autographs, unsigned and mostly undated, are written in ink on odds and ends of music manuscript paper, occasionally using versos of discarded drafts of other works; many show revisions, including some interesting cancelled passages quoted below. Copyist's queries or added accidentals appear there in blue pencil; the latter are tacitly adopted here provided that they are musically coherent.

Each of the official Conservatoire copies forms a bifolio headed on the first recto, and again on the first verso above the musical text, with date and occasion(s) of use; the music occupies the inner facing pages, each copy specifying voice type and "Piano". (The only exception is a copy of just the vocal line of no. [xi], listed below.) Some pencil annotations correct miscopied notes and list dates of later reuse. On reuse, clef changes were sometimes amended; such changes are not noted below. Apart from no. [28], the only source phrasing or breathing indications appear in no. [20], the only dynamic marking in no. [23].

Variants

v. = voice | pf. = piano | LH = left hand | RH = right hand

[1] Admission, 3 November 1910 (men)

Sources: **A**; **C**. No clef changes

[2] Concours, 11 June 1913 (men)

Reused: Admission 1917 (men), Admission 1935, Concours 1937

Sources: **A**; **C1** (1913); **C2** (1917)

A indicates clef changes above vocal staff

Bar 9, pf. Sources give RH as 2 single-stemmed ♩ chords, outer voices tied in addition to present slur (editorially re-notated for clarity)

Bar 12, pf. Sources stem 2 lowest notes of RH chord 1 and lowest note of chord 2 downwards (editorially single-stemmed for consistency)

[3] Admission, October 1907 (men)

Reused: Admission 1911 (men)

Sources: **A**; **C1** (1907); **C2** (1911); **C3** (1911). No clef changes

C1–3 are in B♭; no official copy survives in the autograph key of C. **C1** is explicitly indicated for low voice, the vocal line in 𝄢. **C2** omits this specification and gives vocal line in 𝄞 throughout (as if for high voice), suggesting that **A** had then been overlooked and any 1907 official copy for high voice lost. **C3** (again indicated for low voice) is identical with **C1**

[4] Admission, 8 November 1909 (men)

Sources: **A**; **C**. No clef changes

In **A** this follows the women's test in the 2-page autograph described for no. [11]. Annotations by Fauré in blue pencil indicate that the low-voice version was to be given in 𝄢, in the same key, "pour le 8 9bre [novembre] 09". Visible reworkings include the present bars 15–22, replacing the deleted reading shown below

Bars 17–18, v. Tie in C only

Bar 20, both. **C**: *Rall.* at beat 1; omitted here as it seems uncharacteristic of Fauré's habits (except in unusual cases like the end of no. [26])

Original ending in **A** (showing some reworking):

[5] Examination, 7 January 1908 (men)

Reused: Examination January 1913 (men)

Sources: **A**; **C1** (1908); **C2** (1913). No clef changes

Bar 17, pf. RH chord 2 as in C1–2; **A** single-stems it

[6] Concours, 11 June 1913 (women)

Reused: Concours 1934

Sources: **A**; **C**. **A** indicates clef changes above vocal staff; not carried into **C**

Bar 12–13, pf. **A** omits tie starts (before a system break); **C** omits ties altogether

[7] Admission, 22 October 1908 (men)

Reused: Admission 1912 (men)

Sources: **A**; **C1** (1908); **C2** (1912). No clef changes

A follows the women's test on the single manuscript page described for no. [22]. Autograph annotation indicates that the low-voice version was to be given in 𝄢, in the same key

[8] Examination, 7 January 1909 (men)

Sources: **A**; **C**

A this follows the women's test on the manuscript described for no. [18], and runs over to a 2nd sheet (the verso of a cancelled draft page for the Fifth Impromptu), where it is followed by the dictations for the same date (see Appendix 2). Clef changes are indicated above vocal staff

[9] Examination, 5 May 1914 (women)

Sources: **A**; **C**

A indicates clef changes above vocal staff

Bar 16, pf. **A** gives RH top note as 𝅝, **C** as 𝅗𝅥 (editorially amended)

Bar 18, pf. RH augmentation dot in **C** only (which stems the 2 voices together, no dot after lower note)

[10] Examination, 5 May 1914 (men)

Sources: **A**; **C**

A indicates clef changes above vocal staff, with autograph bar count (22) at end

Bar 11, pf. ♯ to LH f absent in **A**, pencilled in **C**

[11] Admission, 9 November 1909 (women)

Sources: **A**; **C**. No clef changes

A: 2 pp. comprising this and the men's test [no. 4]; marginal annotation in blue pencil in Fauré's hand: "<u>pour le 9 9bre</u> [novembre] <u>09</u>". Shows signs of revision

Bar 20, pf. **C** gives RH top voice as 𝅘𝅥 (downstemmed with dyad), probably a misreading of **A**

[12] Examination, January 1906 (men)

Sources: **A**; **C**

The vocal line incorporates changing clefs. **A** shows an autograph annotation to make an additional copy "for basses" a minor third lower, using 𝄢 throughout

[13] Examination, January 1906 (women)

Reused: Examination January 1910, 8 January 1916 (women)

Sources: **A**; **C1** (1906); **C2** (1916)

The vocal line incorporates changing clefs. **A** shows an autograph annotation to make an additional copy a [minor] third down, using 𝄡 in place of 𝄡 from the end of bar 12. The outer cover of C1 shows a pencilled annotation to make several more copies with various specified clef changes for the 1916 examination; of these only C2 is traced, with clef changes matching C1

Bar 7–8, pf. RH lower-voice tie in C1–2 only (in blue pencil in C1)

Bar 10, pf. Sources single-stem RH beat 3 dyad upwards; editorially restemmed for polyphonic sense (C1–2 also upstem beats 1 and 2 RH 𝅘𝅥s)

Bar 14, pf. Sources single-stem RH beat 3 upwards (editorially restemmed)

[14] Admission, October 1907 (women)

Reused: Admission 1912, 1915, 1931 (women)

Sources: **A**; **C1** (1907); **C2** (1912); **C3** (1915)

No clef changes in **A**, C1 or C3; in C2 changes to bass clef are indicated in pencil above the vocal staff, with one or two notes notated in the new clef each time. The musical text is otherwise identical in all three fair copies

Bar 8, pf. C1–3 give RH 𝅝 dyad as 𝅗𝅥 and stem the 3 notes of beat 1 together

Bar 9, both. In **A** this initially formed 2 bars (9–10), before Fauré tightened the harmonic motion by deleting the four beats in the middle

[15] Examination, 18 May 1915 (women and men)

Sources: **A**; **C**

Tempo indication in **A** in an unidentified (non-autograph) hand. **A** shows signs of revision: bars 18–21 are deleted in blue pencil and replaced (in ink) with the present 18–21 (see below). Clef changes indicated above vocal staff

Bars 17–21, both. Original (deleted) reading of **A**:

Bar 19, pf. **A** stems RH chord 2 top note separately, **C** stems lowermost note separately from upper 2

[16] Concours, 19 June 1909 (men)

Sources: **A**; **C**

"19 Juin 1909", autograph, beneath last system of **A** and "25m[esures]" added after final double bar. Clef changes indicated above vocal staff

[17] Examination, May 1907 (men)

Sources: **A**; **C**

A contains this on a bifolio that precedes it with the dictations for the same date (see Appendix 2) and the women's test, no. [25]. The vocal line incorporates changing clefs

Bar 35, pf. **C**: last RH ♪ d' not e'; probably a misreading of low-placed e' in **A**

[18] Examination, 7 January 1909 (women)

Sources: **A**; **C**

In **A** this precedes the men's test, no. [8] and the dictations of the same date (see Appendix 2). Clef changes are indicated above vocal staff

Bars 6, 9, pf. Sources downstem bar 6 beat 3 RH d' and bar 9 RH $c'\sharp$ (editorially amended)

Bar 12, v. **C**: Penultimate ♪ a tone lower (f' not g'; **A** is ambiguous); "sol" pencilled above the staff

Bar 26, pf. **C** omits RH g', probably the result of emendations on **A** that leave the bar slightly unclear. Sources show RH a'–c' dyad on a single upstem (also the result of emendations); editorially amended to show polyphonic sense

[19] Concours, 13 June 1908 (men)

Sources: **A**; **C**

A indicates clef changes above vocal staff. Tempo indication in **C** only

[20] Concours, 12 June 1912 (women)

Reused: Admission 1937 (women)

Sources: **A**; **C**

A shows the autograph date "12 juin 1912" (bottom of page) and signs of reworking (bars 10 and 21–22 deleted and replaced). Clef changes indicated above vocal staff. Annotations on **C** indicate that a subsequent copy was made "pour le 5 mai" [year unknown] using 𝄢 and 𝄞 only

Bar 7, pf. Downstem from LH e in **C** only

Bar 8, v. ♮ to b' added to both sources in pencil

Bar 9, v. **A** omits ♮ to b'; added to **C** in pencil

Bars 12, 14, pf. **C** stems bar 12 c' with 2 notes above it (as a ♩); both sources notate equivalent 𝅝 d' in bar 14 as ♩‿♩

Bars 13–14, v. Both sources start new slur from bar 14 note 1 (new system in **A**); editorially amended (cf. bar 11)

[21] Examination, 7 January 1908 (women)

Reused: Examination January 1913 (women) and December 1915 (instrumentalists, "Examen spécial")

Sources: **A**, **C1** (1908), **C2** (1913)

No clef changes in **A** or **C2**. **C1** shows a pencilled annotation to make new copies for the Special Examination of December 1915, incorporating changing clefs; these are indicated in pencil above the vocal staff. **C1** also shows the tempo heading "Lento" pencilled at bar 1; this too was probably added for the 1915 examination (perhaps because of the changing clefs)

Bar 21, both. **A** shows beat 3 (pf.) originally as an F^7 chord in root position, followed by a ♩. B♭ chord (bar 22) under a v. $b'\flat$ to end the piece; amended to present ending

[22] Admission, 23 October 1908 (women)

Sources: **A**; **C**

A is on a single page comprising this (systems 1–3) and the men's test (systems 4–6). No clef changes in either source

Bar 15, pf. Sources upstem RH a' and $g'\sharp$ with tied b' (editorially amended)

Bar 18, pf. Sources single-stem RH beat 1, then stem beat 3 f' up with the g' (editorially amended)

[23] Concours, 16 June 1915 (women)

Sources: **A**; **C**

A shows signs of revision and indicates clef changes above vocal staff. The tempo heading and bar 1 $\boldsymbol{p}$ for v. appear in pencil (autograph). The bottom of the page shows an autograph fugue subject and tonal answer in blue ink (unrelated to the test), deleted in pencil

[24] Concours, 14 June 1916 (women and men)

Sources: **A**; **C**

A (see Facsimile, p. V) is headed "H. et F.", shows signs of revision, and indicates clef changes above vocal staff. **C** indicates just "Chanteurs F."; its vocal line omits the last clef change, "fa" [𝄢], at bar 15 beat 4: from bar 14 beat 3 to the end it remains in 𝄞

Bar 7, pf. **C** single-stems chord 1 as ♩

Bar 13, pf. Sources give RH dyad on beat 1 as 𝅝 (editorially amended)

Bar 15, v. Sources give first note of beats 1 and 2 as ♪. [sic]

Bar 17, pf. Fermata to LH dyad in **C** only

[25] Examination, May 1907 (women)

Sources: **A**; **C**

In **A** this follows the dictations of the same date (see Appendix 2) and precedes the men's test, no. [17]. Signs of revision (along with a marginal doodle) include harmonic reworking in bars 4, 7 and 15. The vocal line incorporates changing clefs

Bar 8, pf. Both sources give RH beat 3 on a single upstem; editorially amended for polyphonic sense

Bars 18–20, v. **A** shows both 8ve readings on the same staff, omitting to complete the lower 8ve *ossia* in bar 19 (new page); completed editorially. **A** also shows a deleted earlier reading of vocal line (piano part blank), ending the piece:

[26] Concours, 19 June 1909 (women)

Sources: **A**; **C**

A indicates clef changes above vocal staff. Tempo indication in **A** in copyist's hand

Bar 19–20, pf. **C** omits RH tie

[27] Concours, 13 June 1908 (women)

Sources: **A**; **C**

A indicates clef changes above vocal staff. Tempo indication in **C** only

[28] Vocalise-Étude

A Autograph score used for engraving **E** below: Bibliothèque nationale de France, Paris, Music dept, Ms. 17785. The music, occupying 5 recto sides, is headed (not in Fauré's hand): *Vocalise-Etude / p^r voix élevée / Etendue*. The same hand has amended Fauré's autograph tempo indication *Andante molto moderato* to the present *Adagio molto tranquillo* (retaining the original autograph metronome indication) and added "Gabriel Fauré" after the final double bar. Other publisher and engraver annotations include "gravé [engraved] 31/1-07". Bar 26 is followed by several deleted bars (see below). The only indicated dynamics are *p* at bars 16 and 27 and ⟨⟩ in bar 26

E First edition, as no. 1 (pp. 1–3) in *Répertoire Modern de Vocalises-Etudes / publiées sous la Direction de A. L. Hettich, / Professeur au Conservatoire / 1er volume*, A[lphonse] Leduc, Paris, 1907, A.L. 13,793. The prefatory vocal range is shown as *b–g″* (cf. note below to bar 26). Dynamics and articulation present only in **E**, along with some clarified stemming, are tacitly adopted in the present edition, any exceptions being listed below. In 1934 Leduc issued a low-voice edition in d, with some added cautionary accidentals (tacitly incorporated here) and just one musical variant (in bar 29); the present edition flags the latter as a query, given its uncertain source

Bars 2, 4, 27, 29, v. Sources show breathing commas without parentheses; parentheses added editorially in accordance with the present edition's technical ethos

Bar 7, pf. Beat 4 voice-leading line editorial

Bar 10, pf. **A** omits ♯ to RH *c′*

Bar 19, pf. Sources stem beat 2 *g′* with *a′* (all notes on upper staff); **A** also stems beat 3 *g′* down with *g*

Bar 20, both. **E**: *cresc.* for v. (leaving its extent undefined; editorially replaced by ⟨⟩), ends pf. ⟨⟩ between ♩s 3 and 4 (editorially trimmed)

Bar 22, both. **E**: *dim.* in place of each present ⟩ (leaving the extent of each undefined; editorially renotated using ⟩)

Bar 26, both. **A** reads as follows (the 2 deleted bars followed by a deleted early version of bars 27–28):

The present *ossia* (as in **E**), while possibly an engraver's misreading, might conceivably have been an amendment at proof to complement the deletion seen above of the following *g″♯*

Bar 29, both. **E**: *Dim.* at ♩4 (as well as a bar later); editorially removed). Beat 3 pf. ♮ according to 1934 low-voice edition of **E**, provenance uncertain

[29] Examination, May 1907 (women instrumentalists)

Sources: **A**, **C**

A is headed by the autograph inked annotation "instrumentistes. / filles", with "filles" amended in pencil (autograph) to "femmes" and, pencilled above, "Lecture solfège mai 07". Some corrections appear in blue pencil. The end is followed by Fauré's autograph initials "G.F." above the date "Mai 1907". Clef changes are inked above the vocal staff. **C**, its cover marked "Jury", follows the normal format of the Conservatoire copies (copied compactly to fit on 2 pages)

Bar 5, 6, pf. Sources single-stem RH beat 1; editorially restemmed for polyphonic sense

Bar 6, v. Sources first apply ♭ to *g′* at beat 3 (after a system break); ♭ editorially advanced to beat 2

Bar 10, pf. Sources single-stem RH beats 2 and 3; editorially restemmed for polyphonic sense

Appendix 1

[i] Admission, 21 December 1914 (men)

Source: **C**; no clef changes

[ii] Admission, October 1913 (men)

Source: **C**; no clef changes

Bar 11–12, pf. **C** ties *e′* to *e′♭* [*sic*] across barline

[iii] Examination, 2 February 1915 (men)

Source: **C**. Clef changes indicated in pencil above the staff

Bar 16, pf. **C**: RH *c″* ♩ not ♪

[iv] Examination, 7 January 1914 (women)

Reused: Admission 1929

Source: C; no clef changes

[v] Examination, 7 January 1914 (men)

Reused: Admission 1929

Source: C; no clef changes. For low voice; written in 𝄢 throughout. "𝄞 ou 𝄢" added in pencil on first recto

Bar 10, pf. C gives RH dyad on a single stem; editorially amended to match surrounding bars

Bar 13, pf. C gives RH a as ♩‿♩; editorially amended to match surrounding bars

[vi] Concours, 4 June 1914 (men)

Source: C. Vocal line incorporates changing clefs

[vii] Admission, October 1913 (women)

Source: C; no clef changes

Bar 9, pf. C single-stems RH dyads 1–2 (editorially restemmed to match surrounding bars)

[viii] Examination, 6 January 1912 (women)

Source: C; no clef changes

[ix] Examination, 12 January 1911 (men)

Source: C. Vocal line incorporates changing clefs

[x] Admission, 4 November 1910 (women)

Source: C; no clef changes

Bar 12, pf. C has a tie-like slur from RH g' to $g'\sharp$, possibly confusion with bar 11 (editorially removed to avoid visual confusion)

Bar 16, pf. C gives lower note of LH dyad beat 1 as d (doubtless a misreading); editorially amended following harmonic sense

[xi] Concours, 4 June 1914 (women)

Sources: C1; C2 (vocal line only)

Vocal line in C1 incorporates clef changes to 𝄡 at note 2 of bars 7 and 14; the initial notes involved each time are recopied above the staff, respectively in 𝄢 and 𝄞, with "toujours en clé de sol" pencilled above the latter. An annotation on the front cover indicates that a copy is to be made (no date specified) using 𝄞 and 𝄢 only. C2, all in 𝄞, appears on a single manuscript page, not the normal Conservatoire paper or copyist, with no title or other indication

Bar 10, v. C2 gives beat 4 an 8ve higher

[xii] Examination, 12 January 1911 (women)

Source: C. Vocal line incorporates changing clefs

Bars 4–5, pf. C gives middle voice on upper staff until bar 5 ♪1; layout editorially adjusted

[xiii] Examination, 2 February 1915 (women)

Source: C; no clef changes

[xiv] Concours, 12 June 1912 (men)

Source: C. Vocal line incorporates changing clefs. Annotations indicate that a subsequent copy was made "pour le 5 mai" [year unknown, as with no. [20] above] using 𝄢 and 𝄞 only

[xv] Examination, 8 May 1912 (men)

Reused: December 1915 (also instrumentalists)

Sources: C1 (1912); C2 (1912)

Vocal line incorporates changing clefs. C2 shows a pencilled annotation to make six new copies (now untraced) for examination on "mercredi 18 ~~Janvi~~ Décembre 1915" [sic: 18 December 1915 was a Saturday], incorporating additional clef changes, which are shown above the vocal staff in pencil

[xvi] Examination, 8 May 1912 (women)

Source: C. Vocal line incorporates changing clefs

Bar 5, pf. C gives RH dyad 1 a' as ♩ and $c'\sharp$ as 𝅝, then stems d' upwards; durations and stems editorially inverted for harmonic sense

Appendix 2: Dictations

May 1907

A 1st recto of bifolio described above for no. [17]. Under Fauré's overall heading "Dictées", "Exam Mai 07" is added in pencil, the tests then indicated respectively "chanteurs – femmes", "chanteurs – hommes", "Instrumentistes – filles" and "Instrumentistes – garçons". Under the last one is added: "2 lignes ~~instrumentistes~~ / chanteurs".

January 1909

A Runs on from men's *solfège* test, no. [8], on the verso of a cancelled draft page for the Fifth Impromptu. Headed by Fauré "Dictée", then respectively "femmes" and "Hommes"

Chronological index of contents

	hommes men	*femmes* women	*hommes et femmes* men and women
January 1906	[12]	[13]	
[1906 or January 1907]			[28]*
May 1907	[17]	[25] [29]**	Dictations
October 1907	[3]	[14]	
7 January 1908	[5]	[21]	
13 June 1908	[19]	[27]	
22–23 October 1908	[7]	[22]	
7 January 1909	[8]	[18]	Dictations
19 June 1909	[16]	[26]	
8–9 November 1909	[4]	[11]	
3–4 November 1910	[1]	[x]	
12 January 1911	[ix]	[xii]	
6 January 1912	—	[viii]	
8 May 1912	[xv]	[xvi]	
12 June 1912	[xiv]	[20]	
11 June 1913	[2]	[6]	
October 1913	[ii]	[vii]	
7 January 1914	[v]	[iv]	
5 May 1914	[10]	[9]	
4 June 1914	[vi]	[xi]	
21 December 1914	[i]	—	
2 February 1915	[iii]	[xiii]	
18 May 1915			[15]
16 June 1915	—	[23]	
14 June 1916			[24]

For January 1912 and the 1915 Concours no men's test piece is identified, nor a women's test for autumn 1914 Admission. Existing tests may have been reused without the fact being noted; for the 1915 Concours the women's test may also have served for men (as in May 1915 and June 1916). The exceptionally late men's exam of December 1914 resulted from war circumstances. Other examinations over these years either used vocalises by others (cf. Preface note 5) or reused ones by Fauré.

* No. [28] did not serve for Conservatoire exams.

** This was Fauré's only vocalise set for sight-singing by instrumentalists rather than singers.